DRAW 50

Creepy Crawlies

The Step-by-Step Way to Draw Bugs, Slugs, Spiders, Scorpions, Butterflies, and Many More . . .

BOOKS IN THIS SERIES

DRAW 50 | Creepy Crawlies

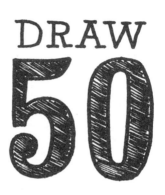

The Step-by-Step Way to Draw Bugs, Slugs, Spiders, Scorpions, Butterflies, and Many More . . .

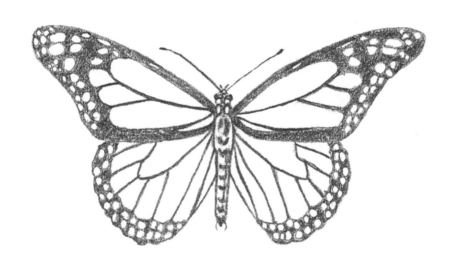

LEE J. AMES
with Ray Burns

Watson-Guptill Publications, New York

Published in the United States by Watson-Guptill Publications,
an imprint of the Crown Publishing Group, a division of Random
House, Inc., New York, in 2013.

www.crownpublishing.com
www.watsonguptill.com

WATSON-GUPTILL and the WG and Horse designs are
registered trademarks of Random House, Inc.

Originally published in hardcover in the United States by
Doubleday, a division of Random House Inc., New York, in 1991.

Library of Congress Cataloging-in-Publication Data

Ames, Lee J.
    Draw 50 creepy crawlies/Lee J. Ames with Ray Burns.—1st ed.
        p.   cm.
    Summary: Step-by-step instructions for drawing fifty different
insects, spiders and other crawling or flying creatures.
    1. Insects in art—Juvenile literature. 2. Animals in art—Juvenile
literature. 3. Drawing—Technique—Juvenile literature. [1. Insects in
art. 2. Animals in art. 3. Drawing—Technique.] I. Burns, Raymond,
1924—   . II. Title III. Title: Draw fifty creepy crawlies.
    NC 783.A44   1991
743'.6—dc20   90-19396
CIP   AC

ISBN 978-0-8230-8614-6
eISBN 978-0-8230-8615-3

Printed in the United States of America

10 9 8 7 6 5 4 3 2 1

Thanks again, Ray,
for sharing with me your wonderful talent.
—L.J.A.

To Lee Ames,
a good friend these many years.
—R.B.

TO THE READER

This is number twenty in our "Draw 50" series. This is the twentieth time I've had the fun and privilege of showing you a way of creating drawings. This time it's the method used by Ray Burns and myself. Working with Ray, and bringing his unique talent to the book, made this a most delightful experience.

Ray is a top illustrator of our time. In your library and bookstore, you will find many books that have been enhanced by his talent. In black and white, in full color, from cartoons to fantasy to realism, from fairy tales to history to natural science, he has shown himself to be an expert. Thank you, Ray, for joining with me in this project!

When you start working, I would recommend you use clean white bond paper or drawing paper and a pencil with moderately soft lead (HB or No. 2). Keep a kneaded eraser (available at art supply stores) handy. Choose the creepy crawly you want to draw and then, very lightly and very carefully, sketch out the first step. Also very lightly and carefully, add the second step. As you go along, study not only the lines but the spaces between the lines. Size your first steps as closely as possible to the lines and the spaces in the book—not too large, not too small. Remember, the first steps must be constructed with the greatest care. A mistake here could ruin the entire drawing.

As you work, it's a good idea to hold a mirror to your sketch from time to time. The image in the mirror frequently shows distortion you might not have noticed otherwise.

In the book, new steps are printed darker than the previous steps. This is so they can be clearly seen. But you should keep your construction steps very light. Here's where the kneaded eraser can be useful. You can use it to lighten a pencil stroke that is too dark.

When you've completed all the steps, and when you're sure you have everything the way you want it, complete the drawing with firm, strong penciling. If you like, you can go over this with India ink (applied with a fine brush or pen), or a permanent fine-tipped ballpoint or felt-tipped marker. When your work is thoroughly dry, you can then use the kneaded eraser to clean out all the underlying pencil marks.

Always remember that even if your first attempts at drawing do not turn out the way you'd like, it's important to *keep trying*. Your efforts *will* eventually pay off and you'll be pleased by what you can accomplish.

I sincerely hope you will improve your drawing skills and have a great time working on these creepers and crawlers.

LEE J. AMES

TO THE PARENT OR TEACHER

In fourth grade, many years ago, we were given an assignment to draw something to honor President Lincoln's birthday. An immediate competition developed among the four or five class artists. Which of us could draw the best portrait of Honest Abe?

We, of course, would not agree that any other one of us did the best. Our pride led each of us to consider himself the winner. Today I couldn't honestly make the judgment call that mine deserved to be number one, but I did learn something that ultimately resulted in the "Draw 50" books.

I learned the importance of peer approval. The encouragement given to us artists by the rest of the class and the praise we gave one another was heady inspiration. Most of the group went on to become successful professionals.

All the drawings of Abraham Lincoln that the class artists made were copied from other sources. This despite general disapproval of "copying." We copied from the Lincoln penny; from a five-dollar bill; from a calendar; and from sale advertisements in the newspaper. We copied someone else's work, stroke by stroke, and we erased and reworked. Many considered this to be a noncreative, harmful way to learn drawing. But we liked what we finally got. Our friends and classmates liked what we did and we were encouraged. We were on a roll, and that was of overriding importance.

Later we were able to learn technique, theory, media, and much more with the gift of incentive provided by friends, classmates, and family. Early on we copied, then we found ways to do our own original things.

Mimicry is prerequisite to creativity!

It is my hope that my readers will be able to come up with drawings that will bring them gratifying approval from friends, classmates, and family. After that I look forward to the competition.

Enjoy!

LEE J. AMES

DRAW
50 CREEPY
CRAWLIES

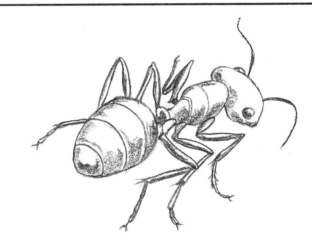

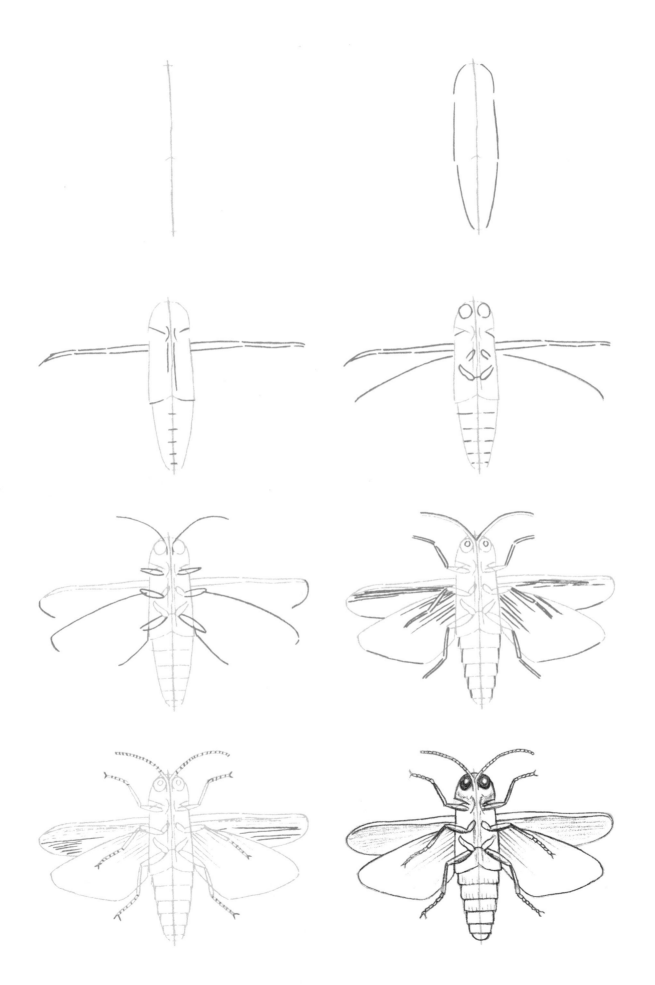

Firefly

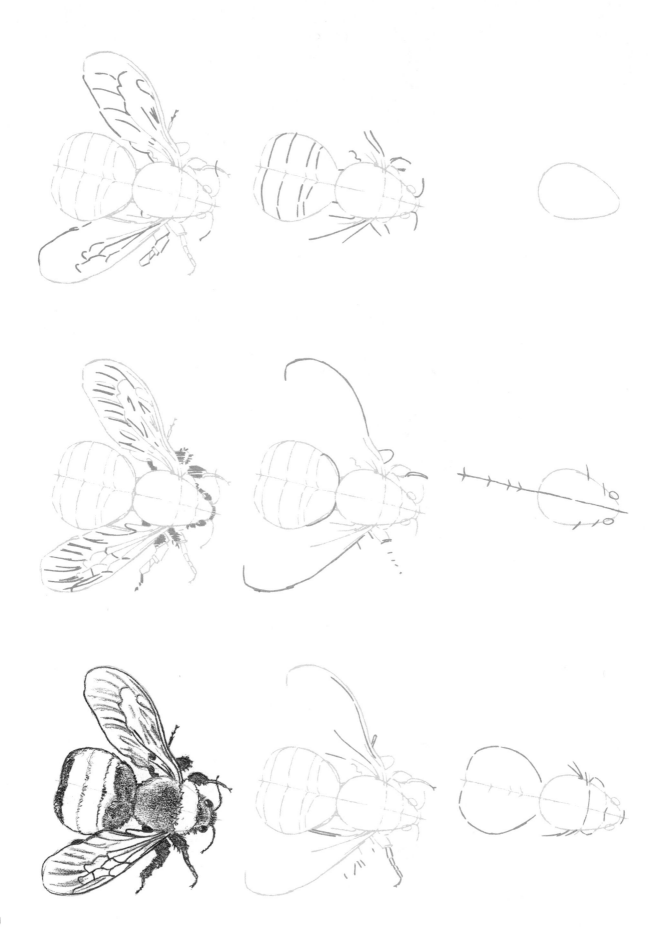

Bumblebee

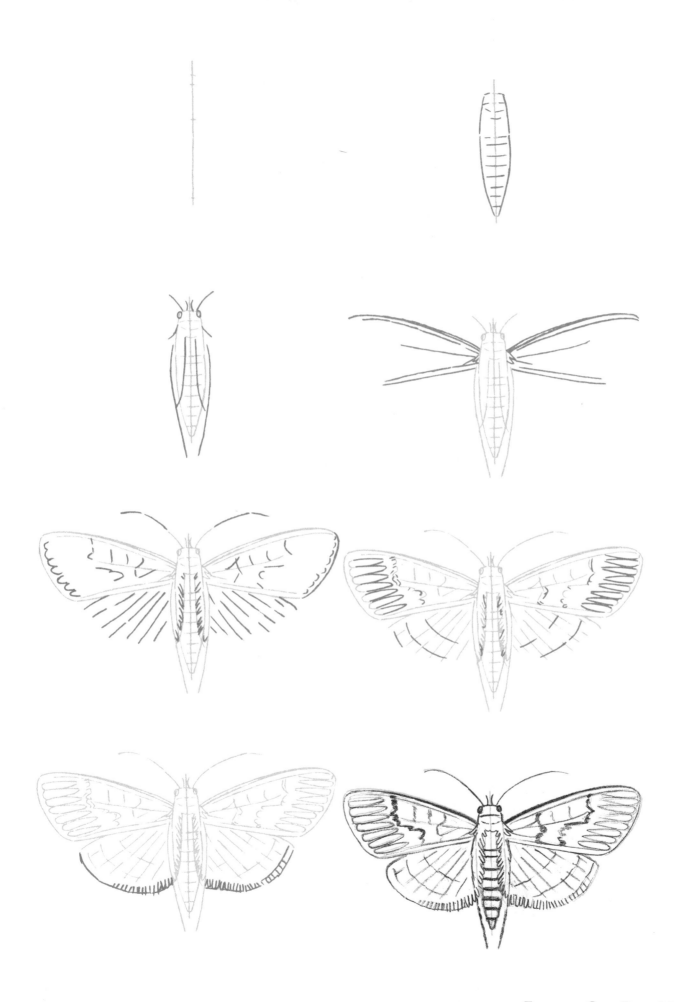

European Corn Borer Moth

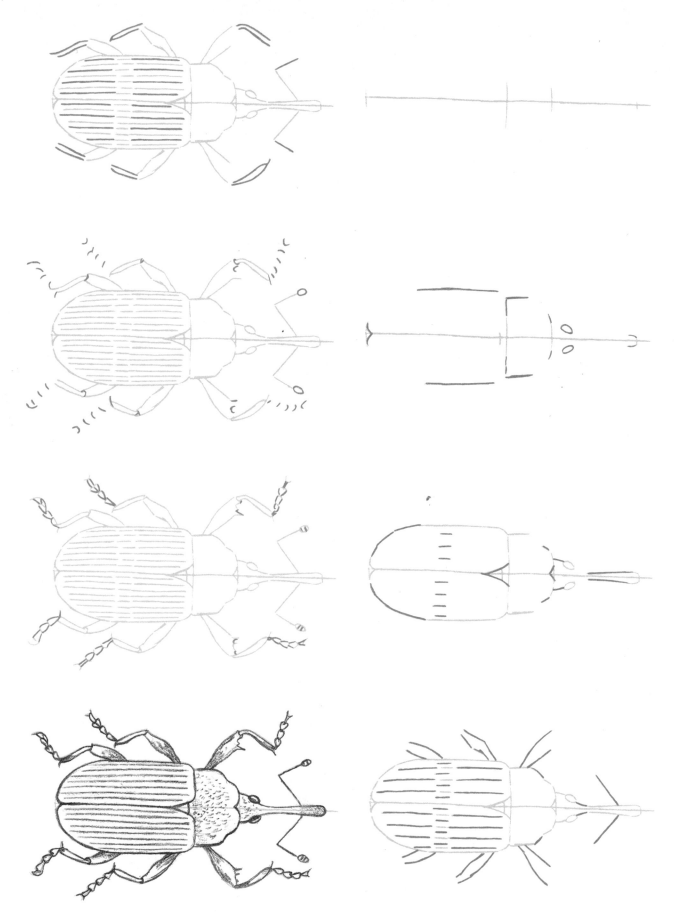

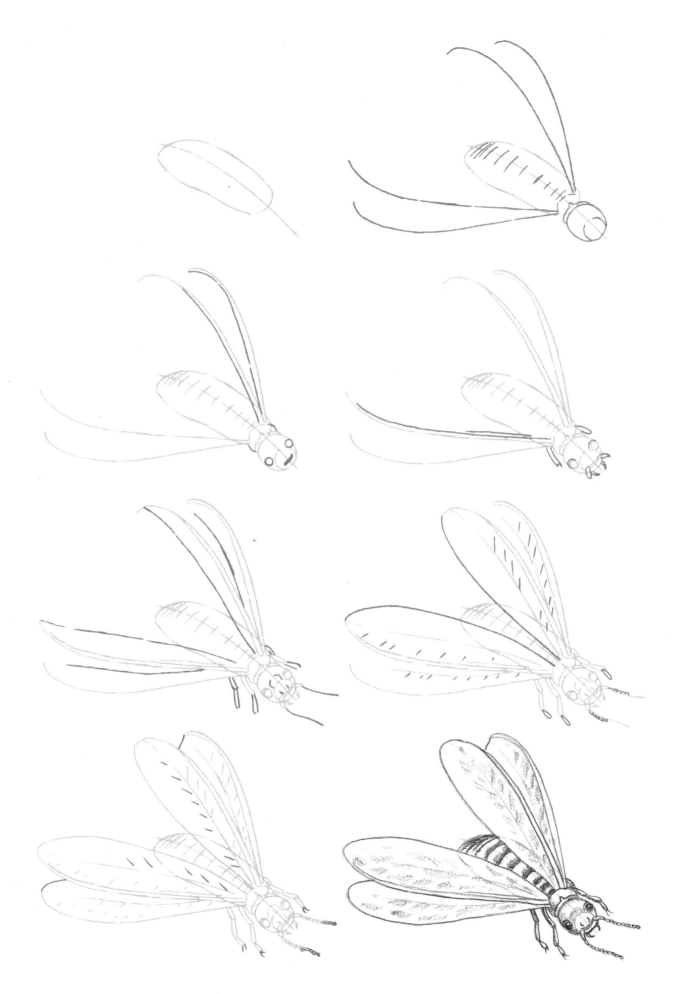

Winged Termite

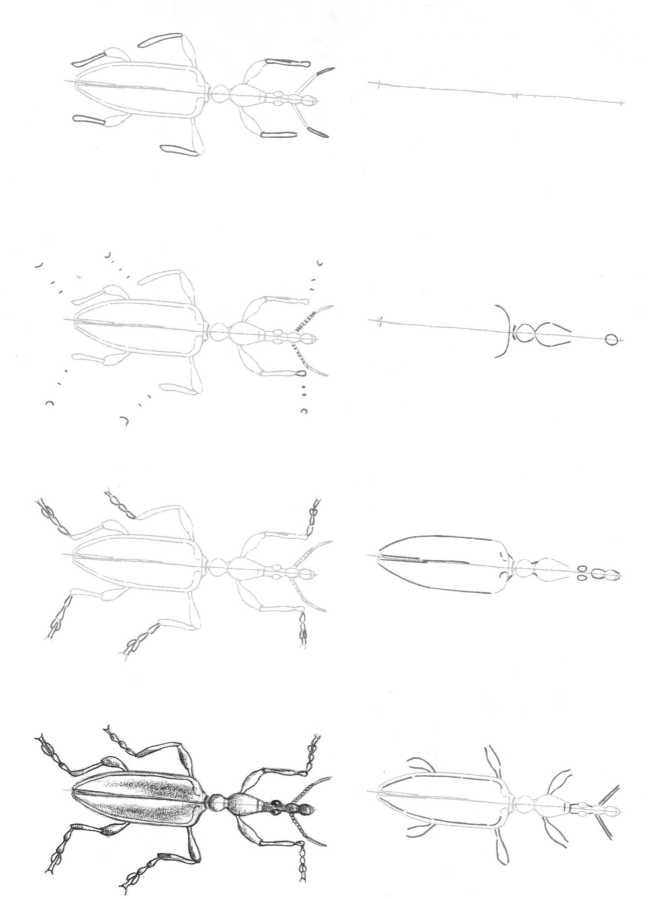

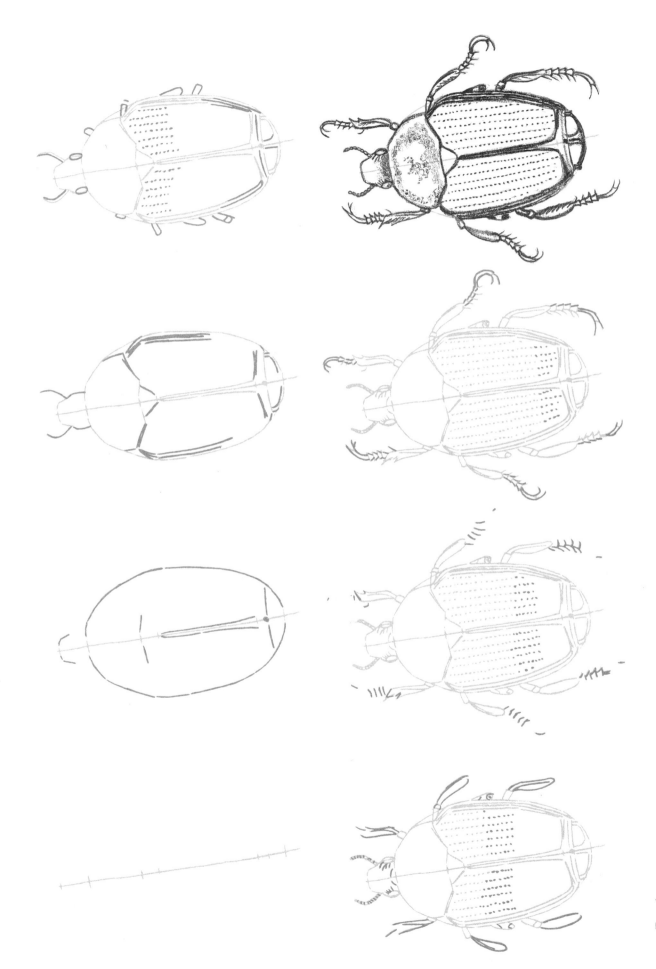

Japanese Beetle

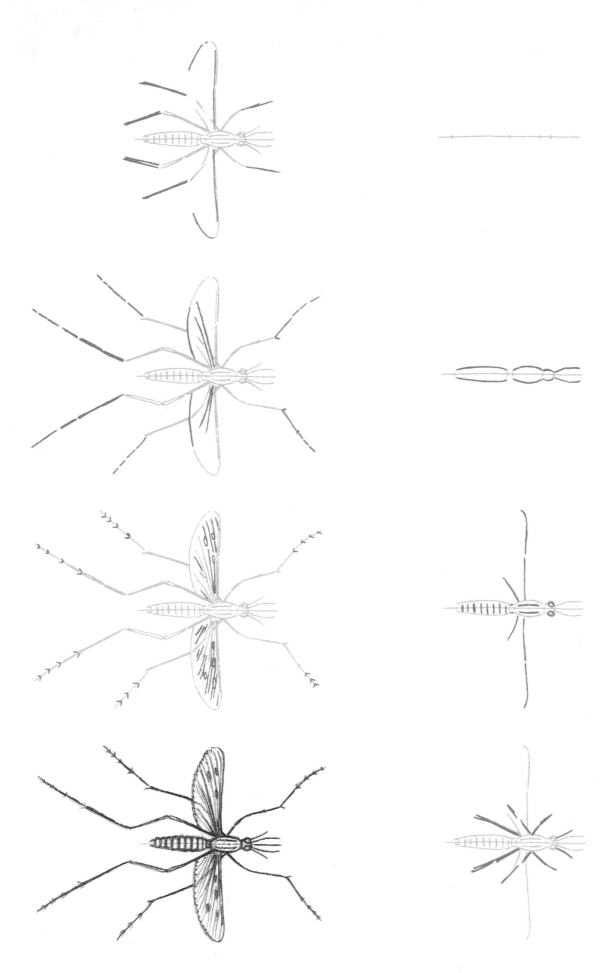

Anopheles Mosquito

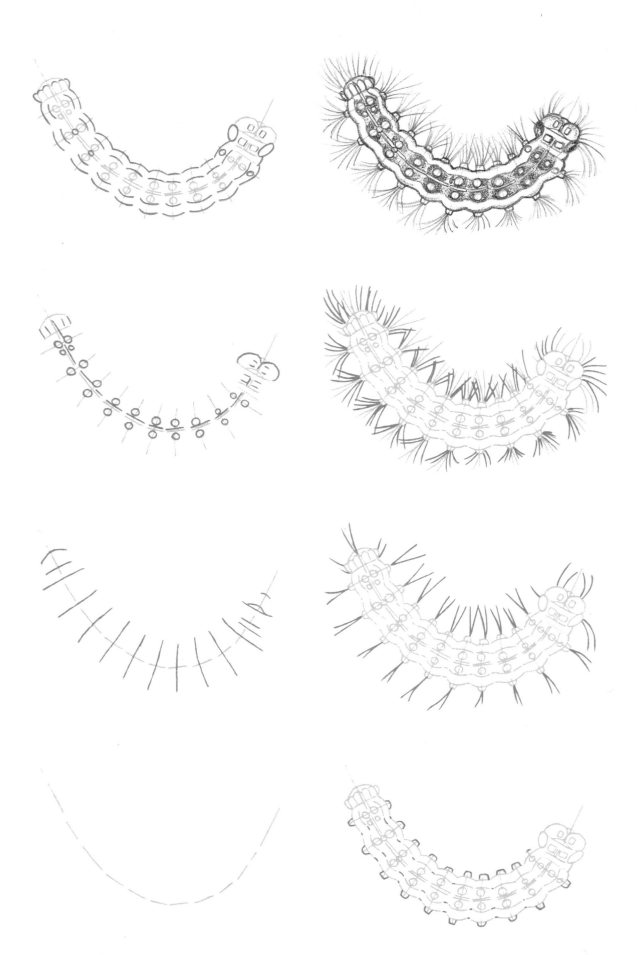

Gypsy Moth Larva

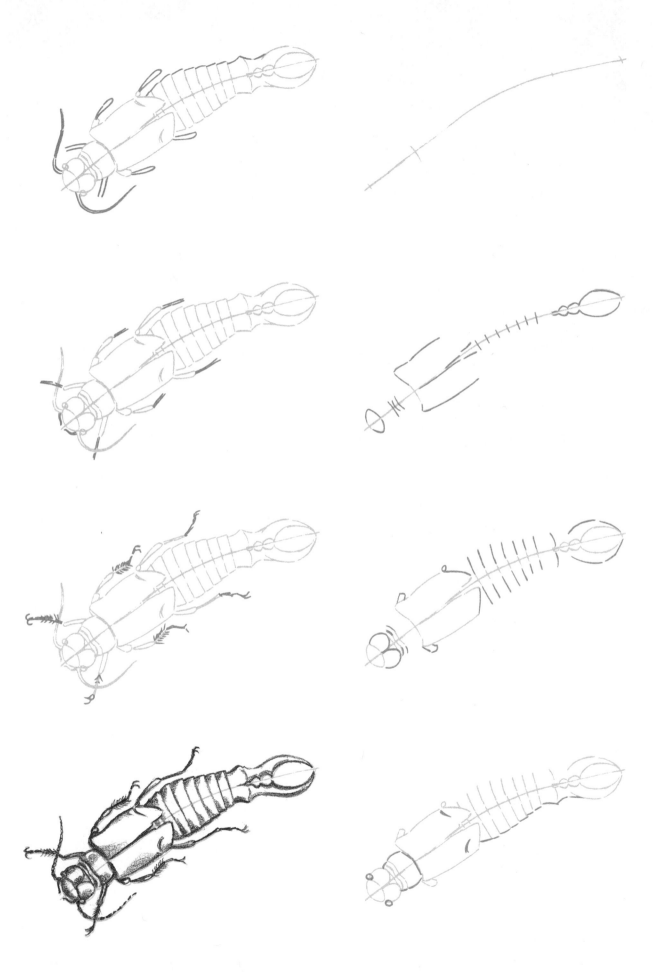

Earwig

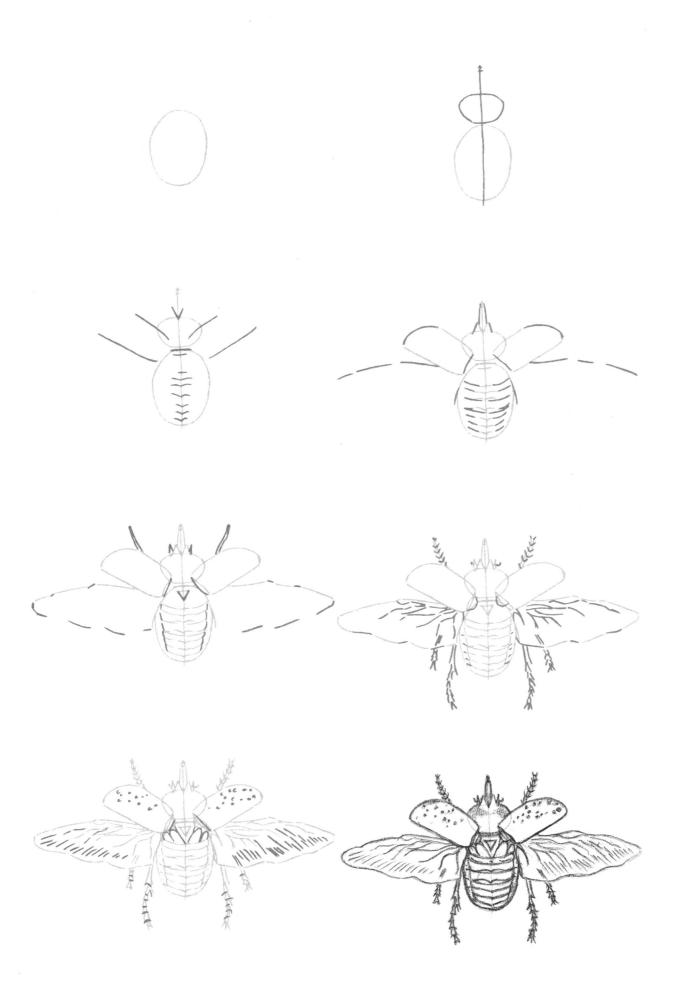

Unicorn Beetle

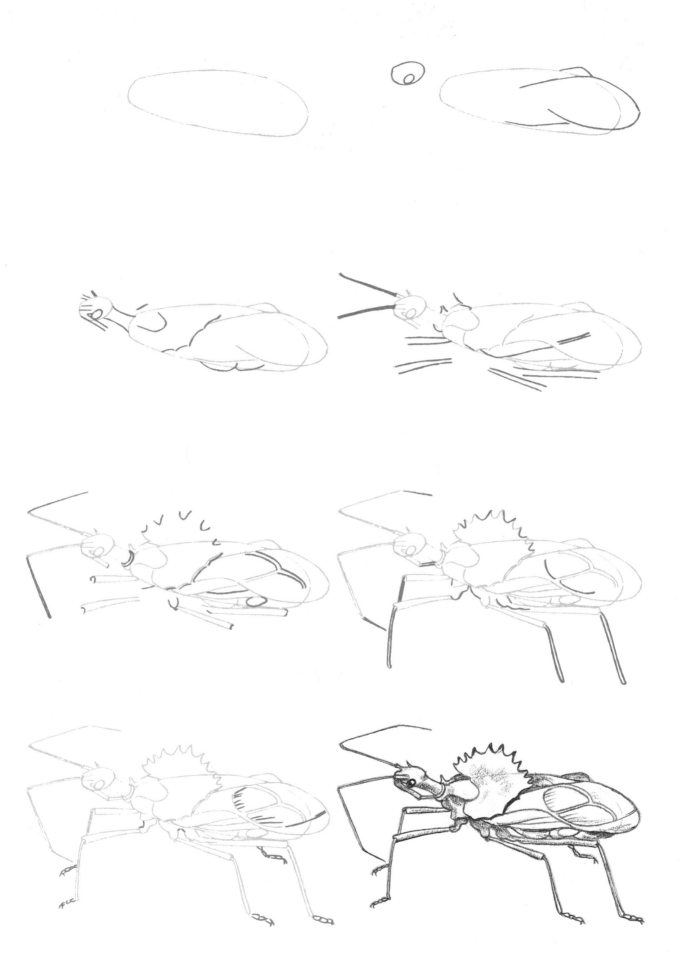

Assassin Bug

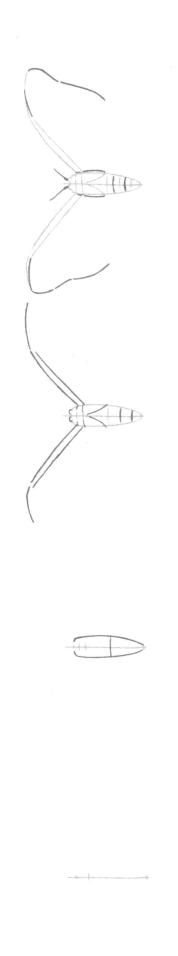
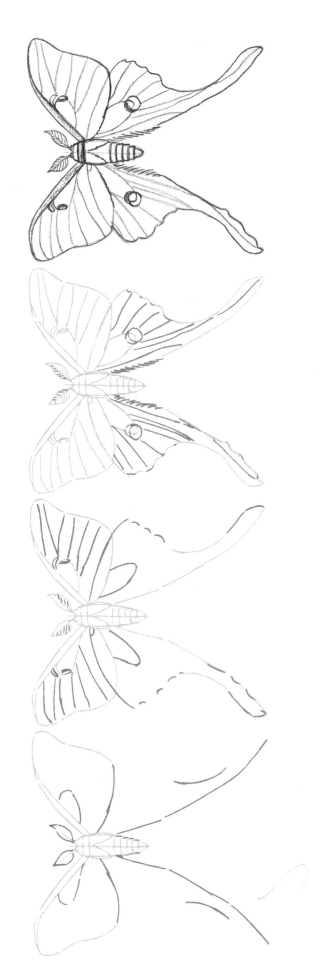

Luna Moth

Walking Stick

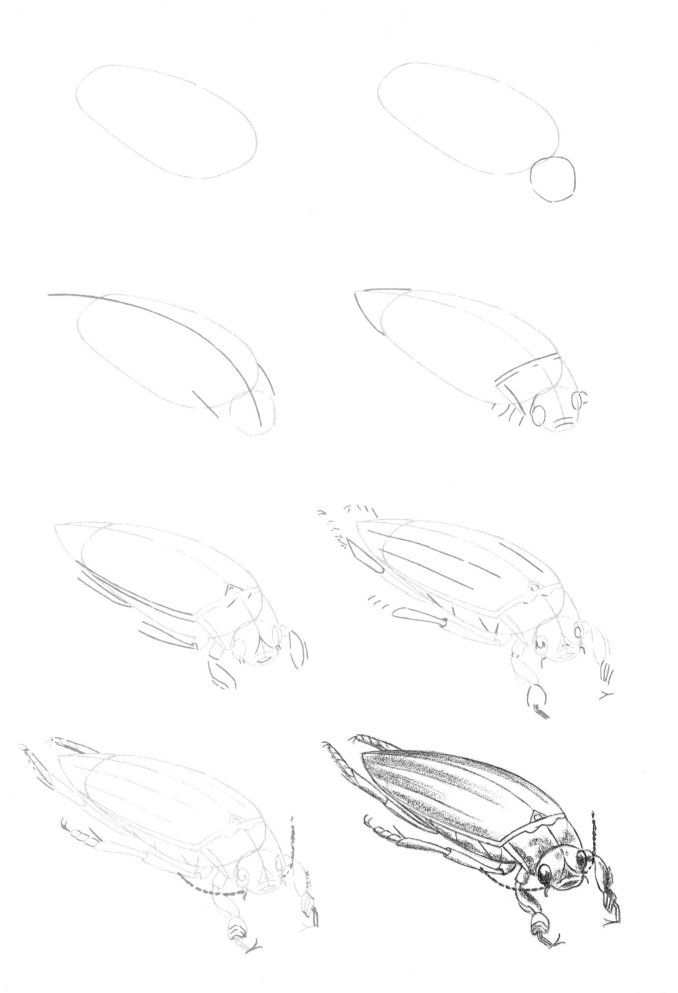

Predacious Diving Beetle

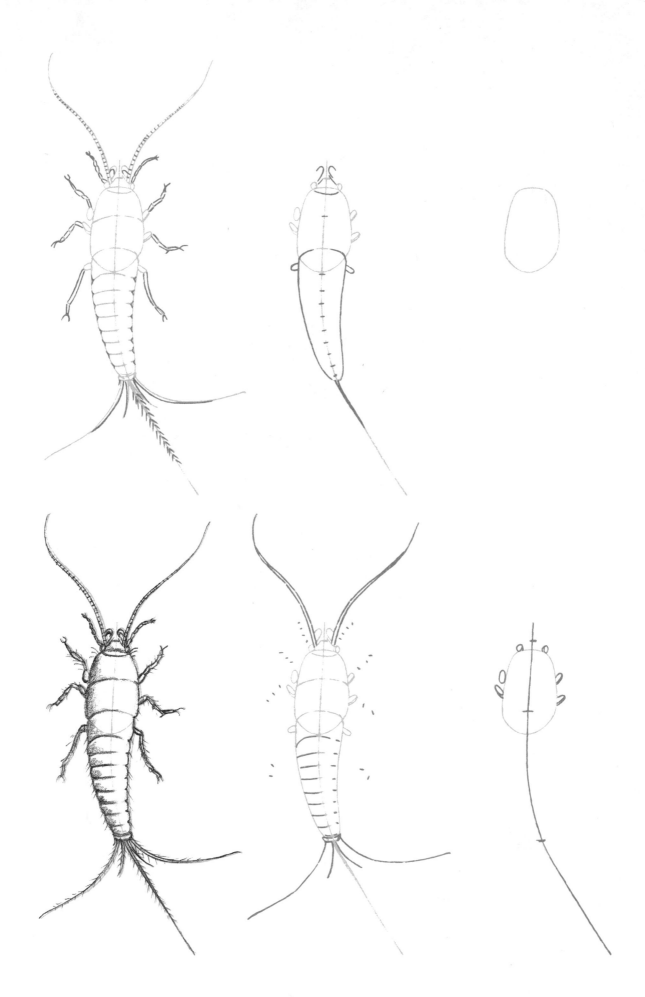

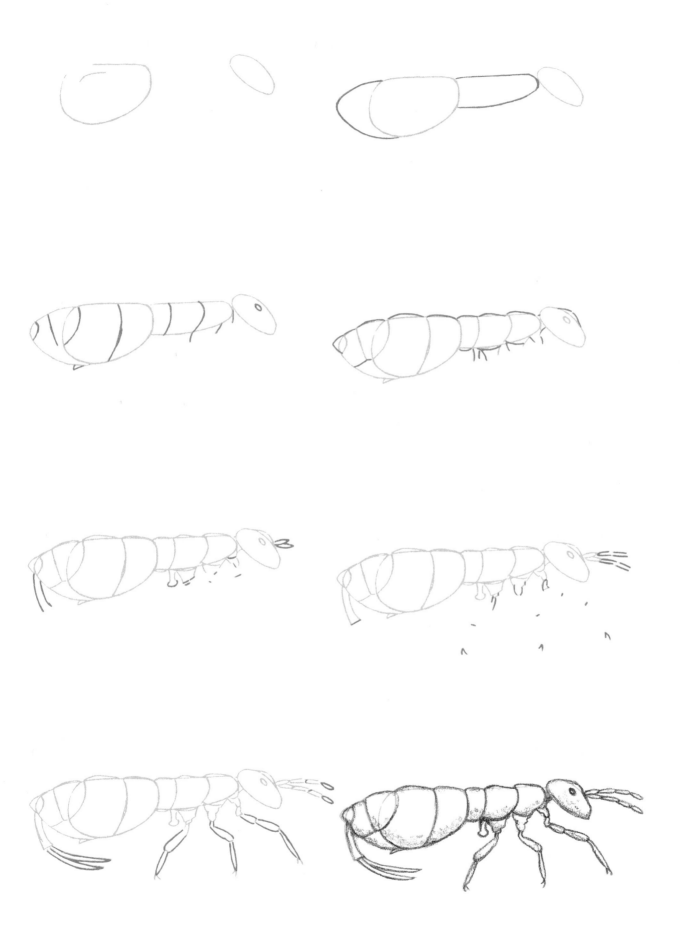

Springtail

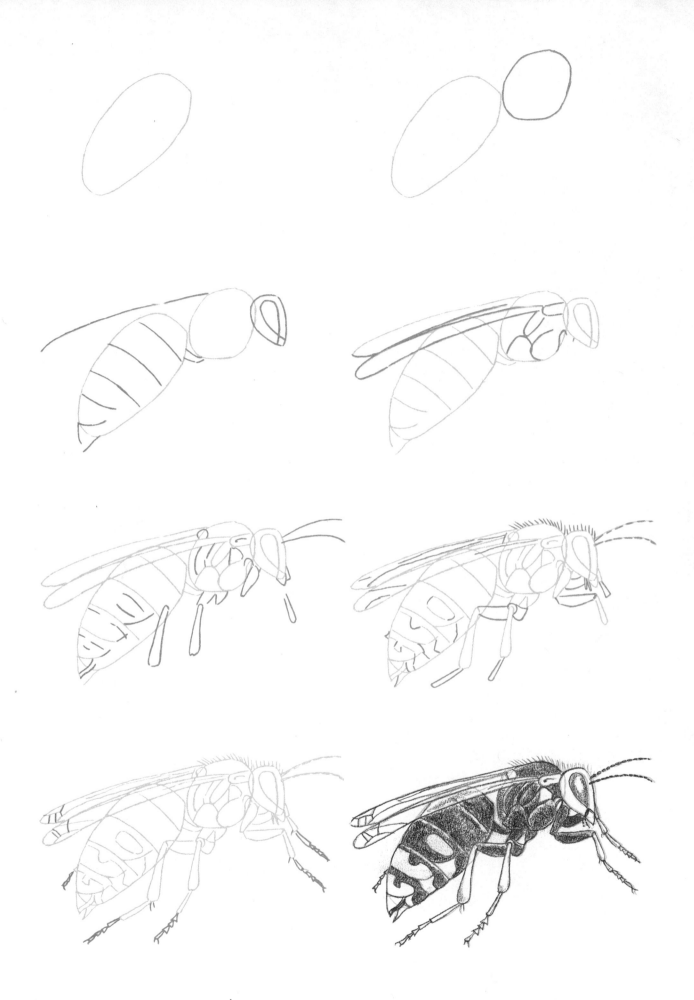

Bald-Faced Hornet

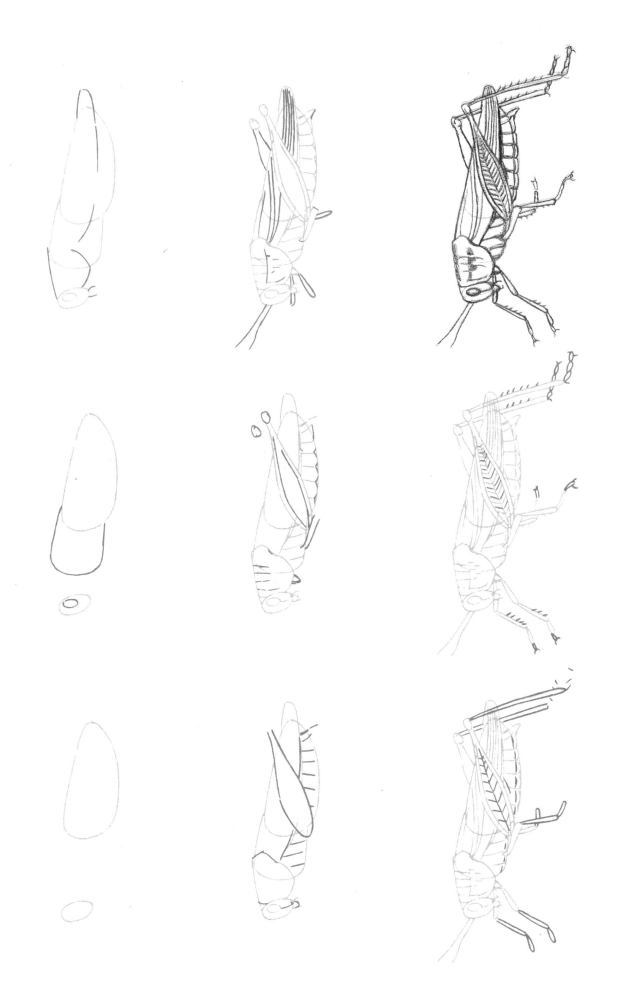

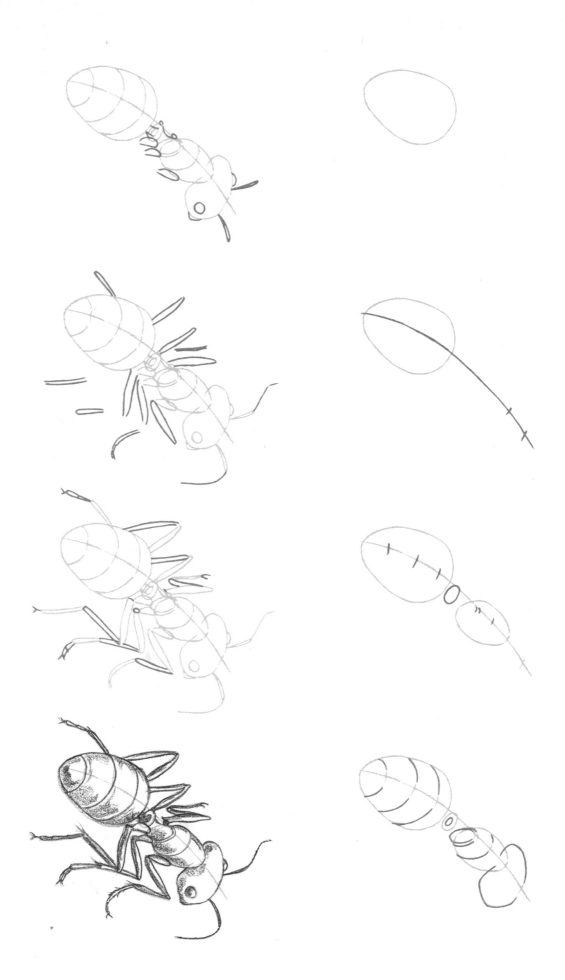

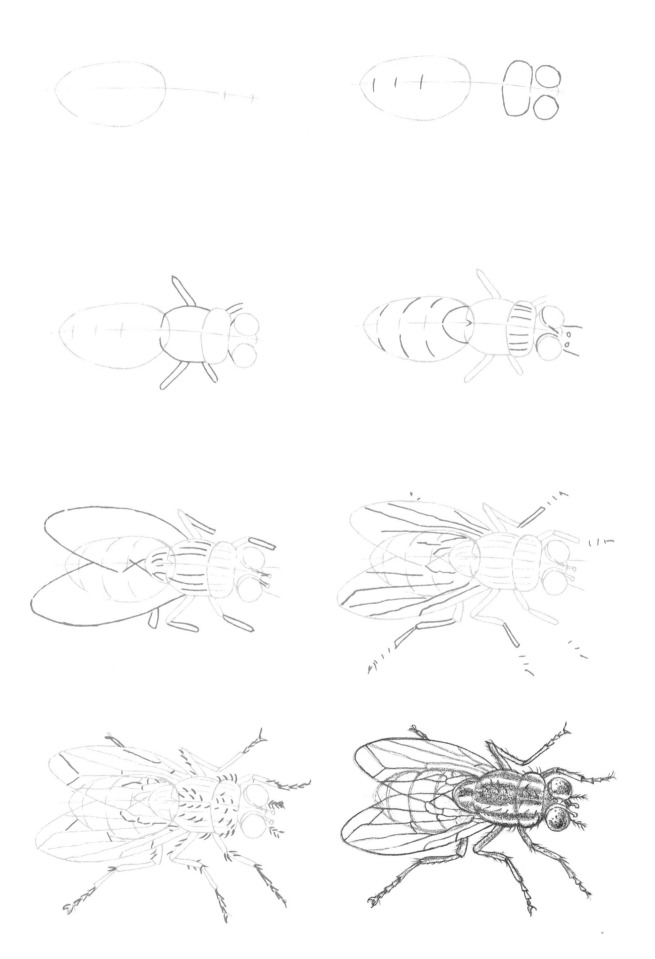

Housefly

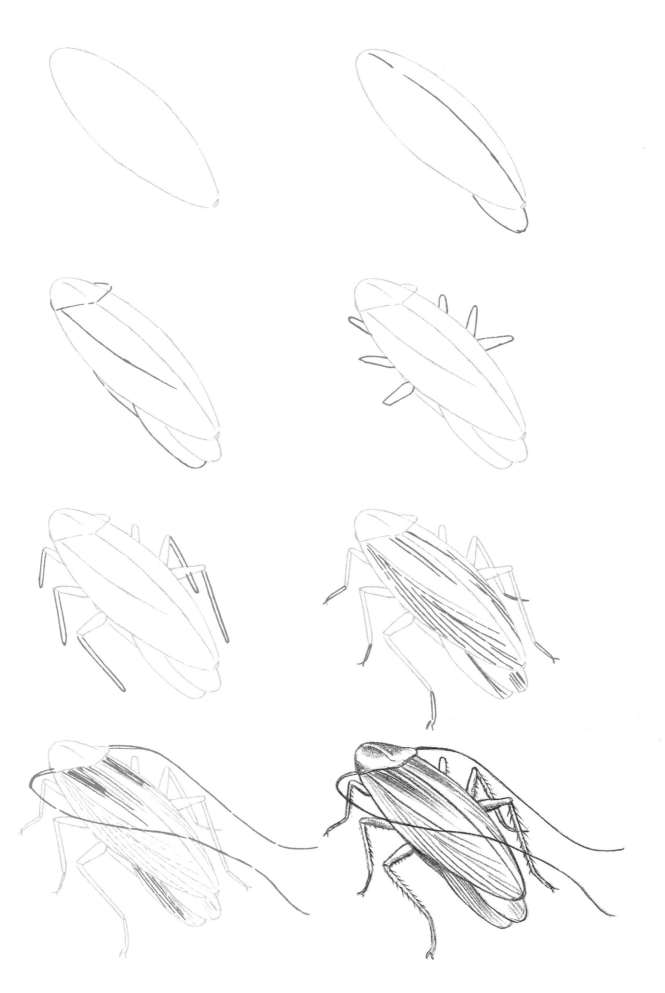

American Cockroach

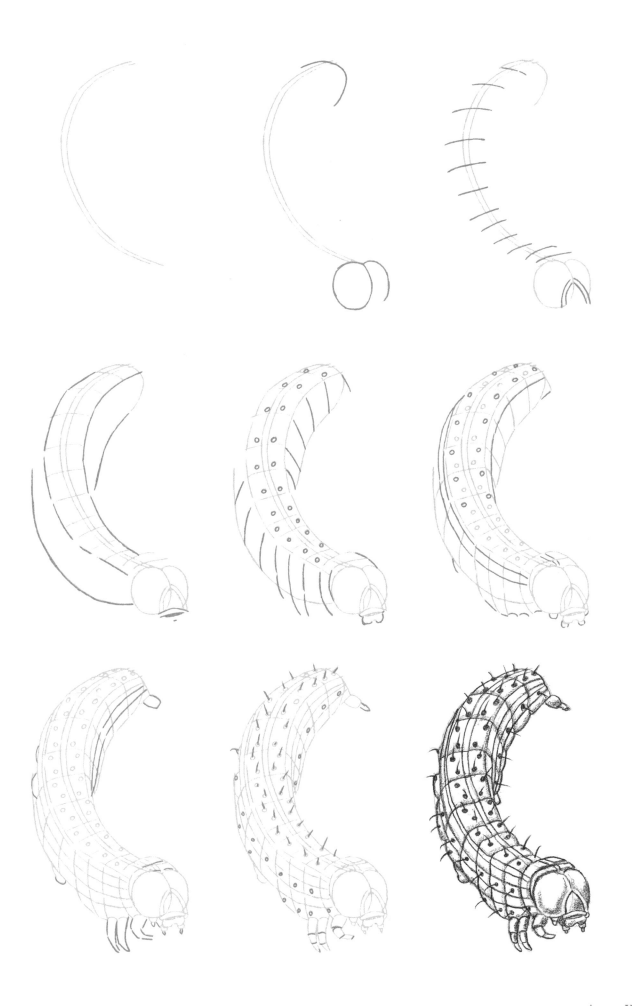

Army Worm

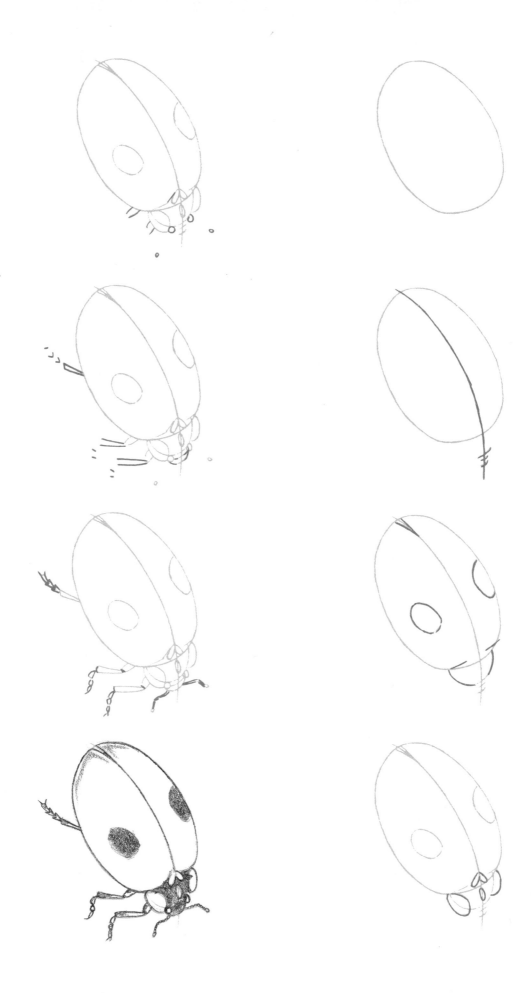

Ladybug

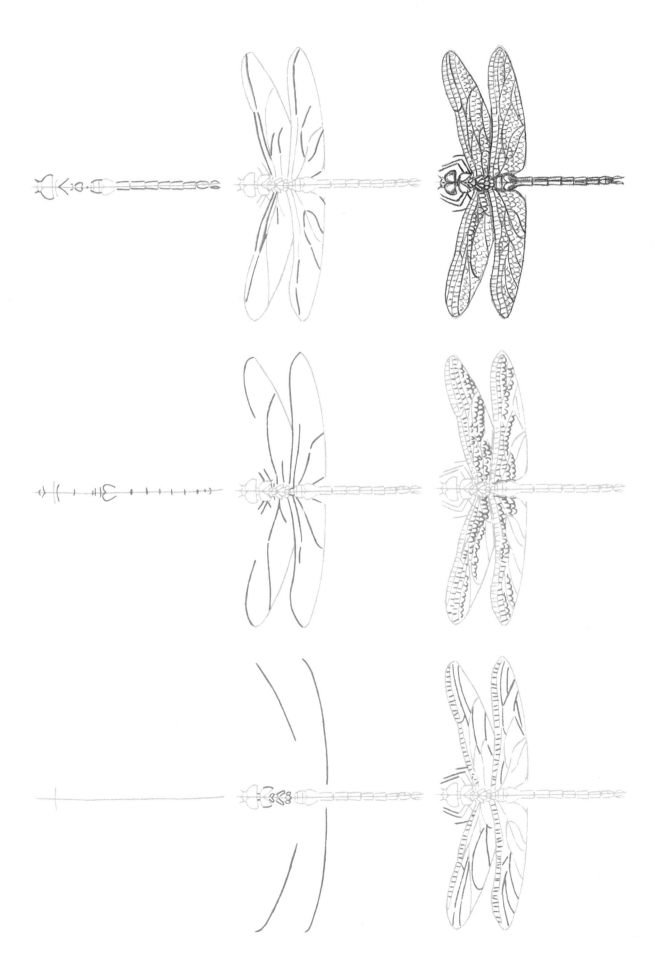

Dragonfly

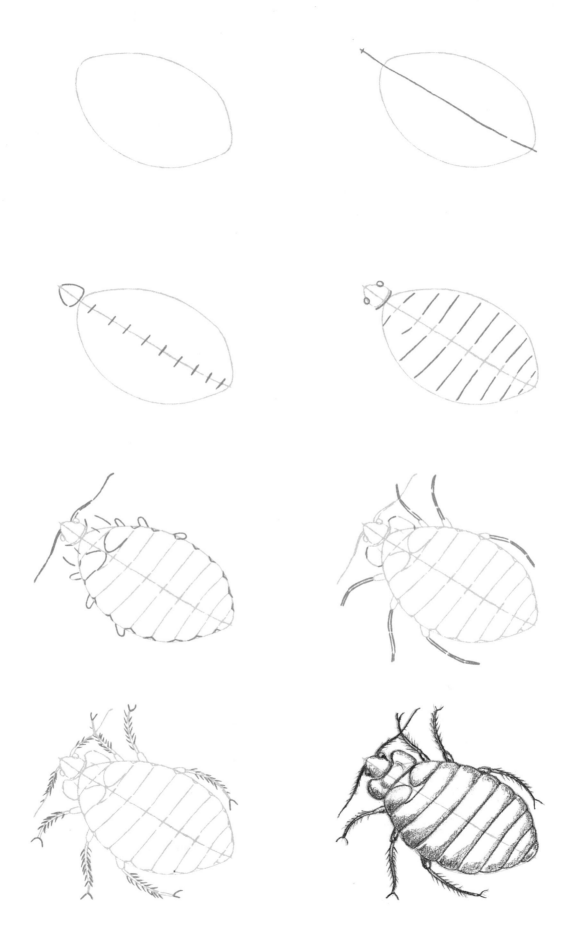

Bedbug

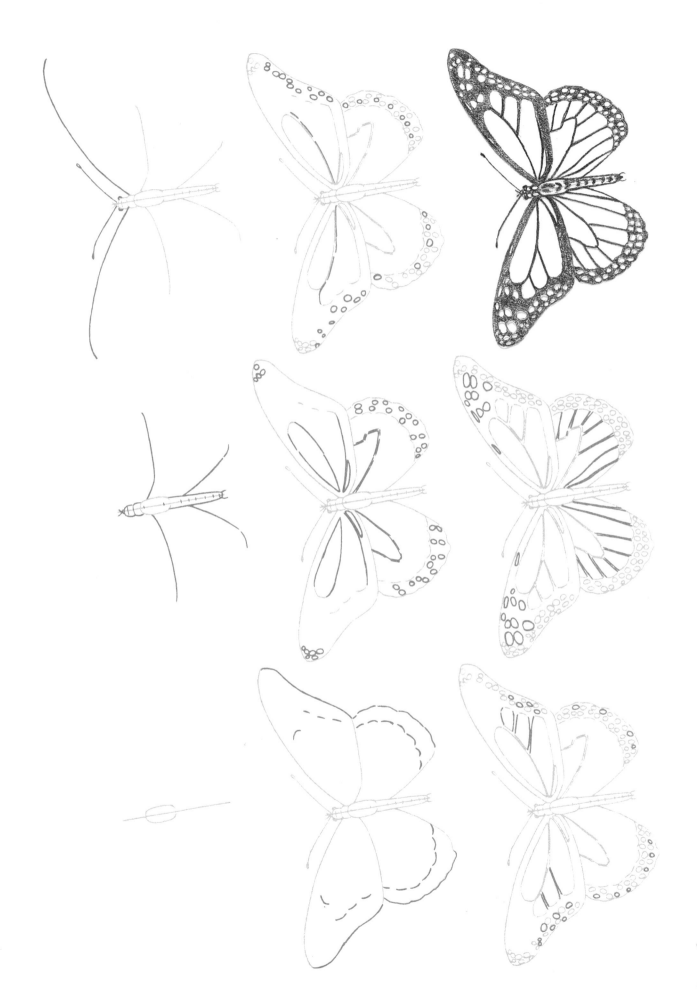

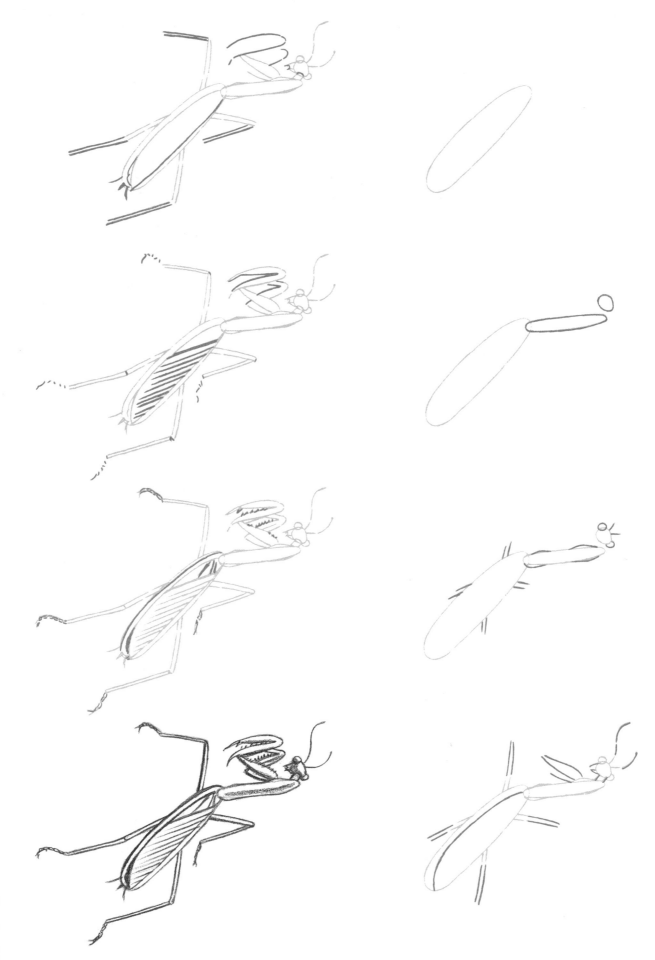

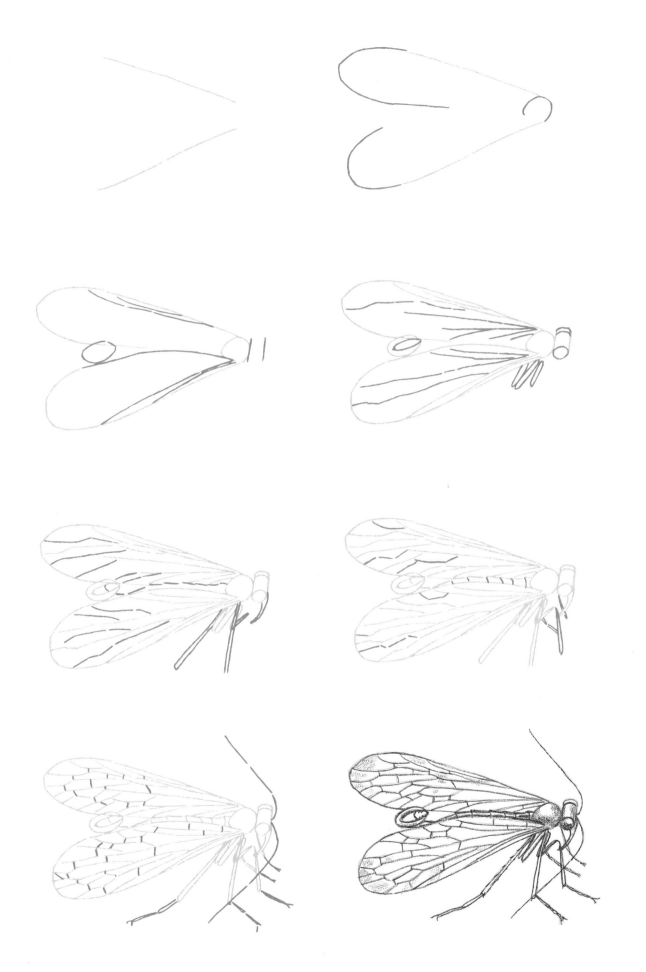

Scorpion Fly

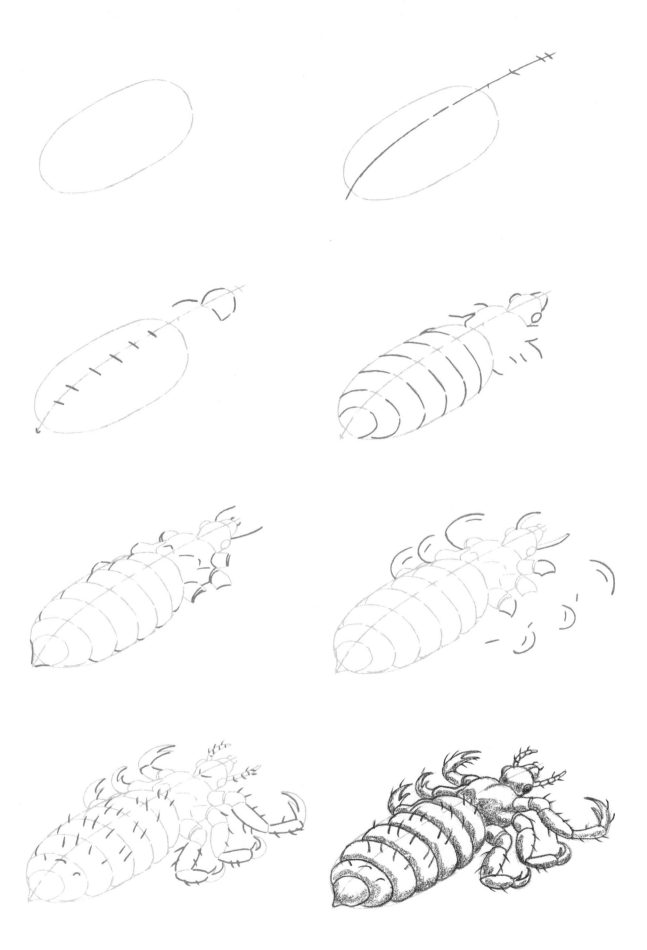

Head Louse

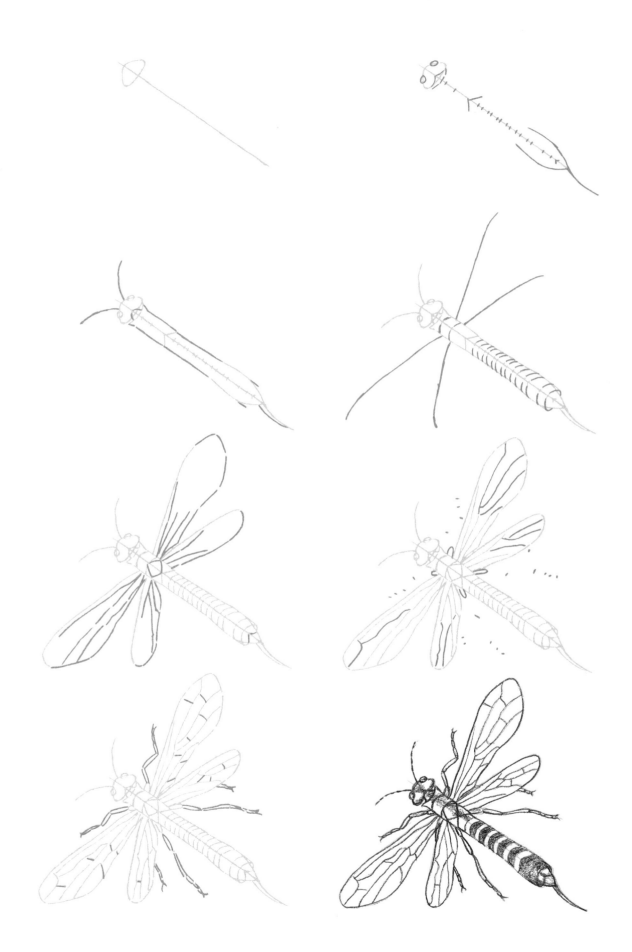

Horntail

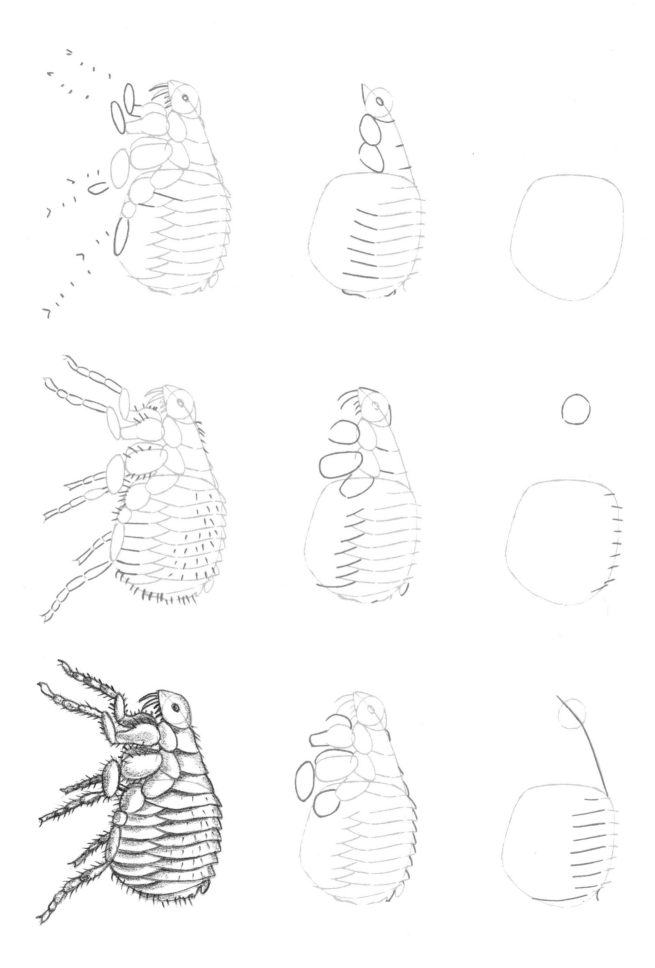

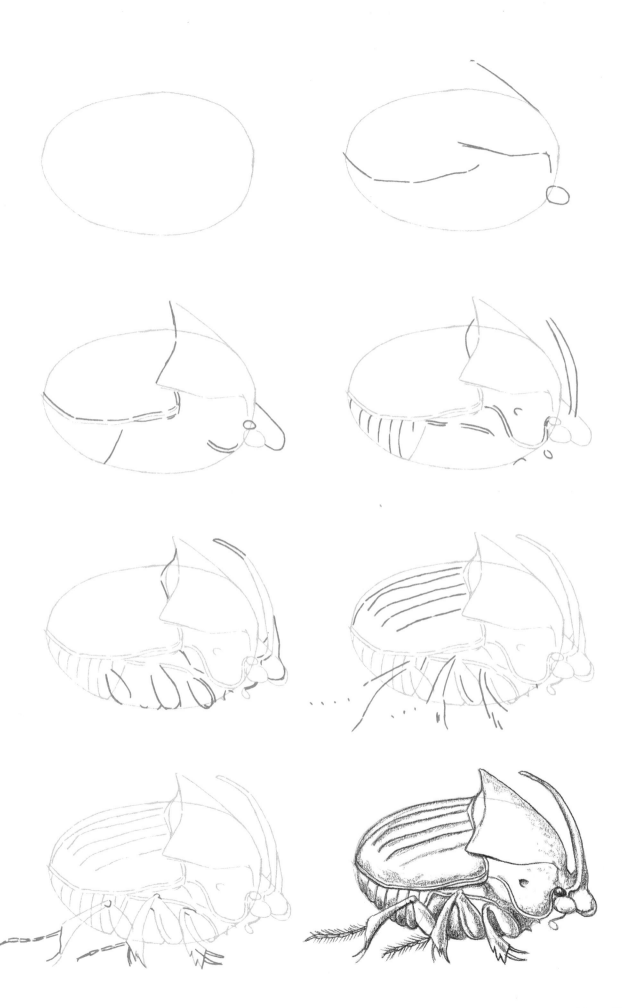

Dung Beetle

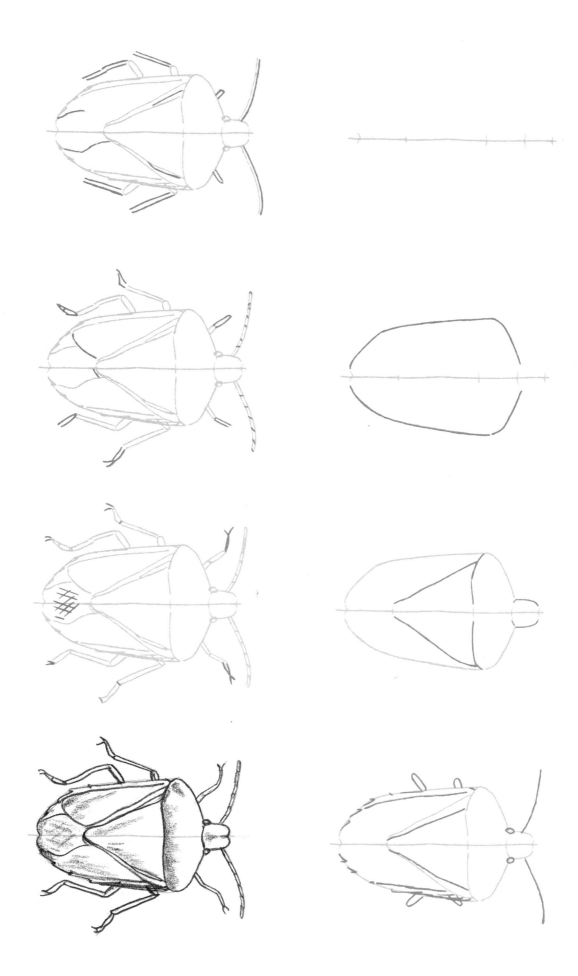

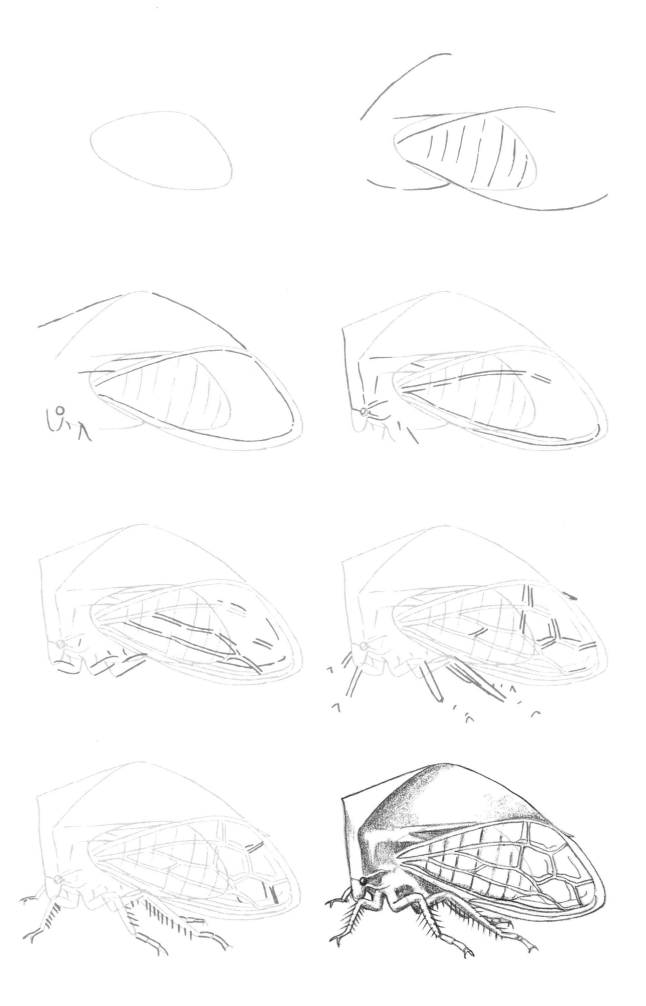

Buffalo Treehopper

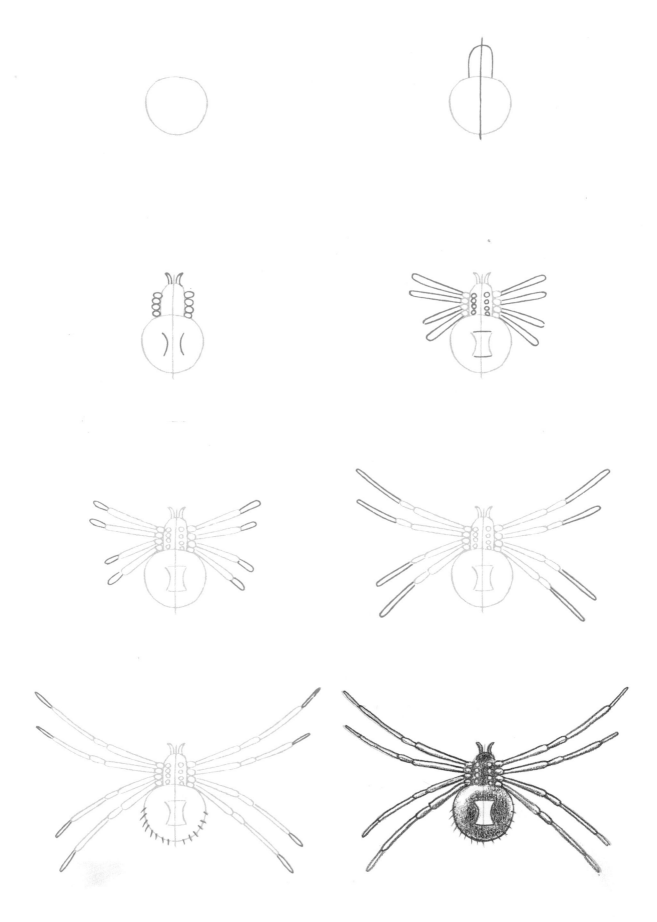

Black Widow Spider

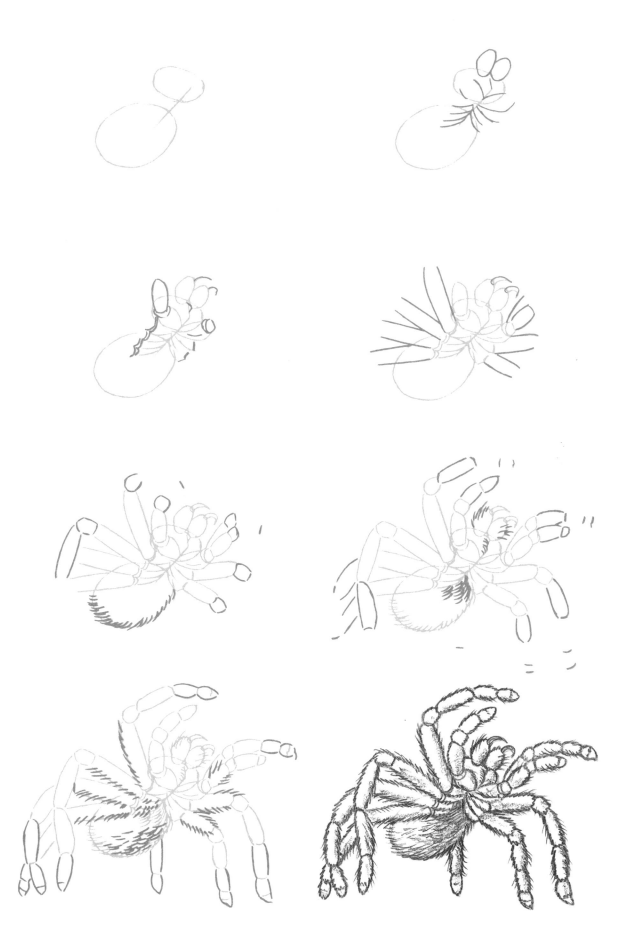

Tarantula

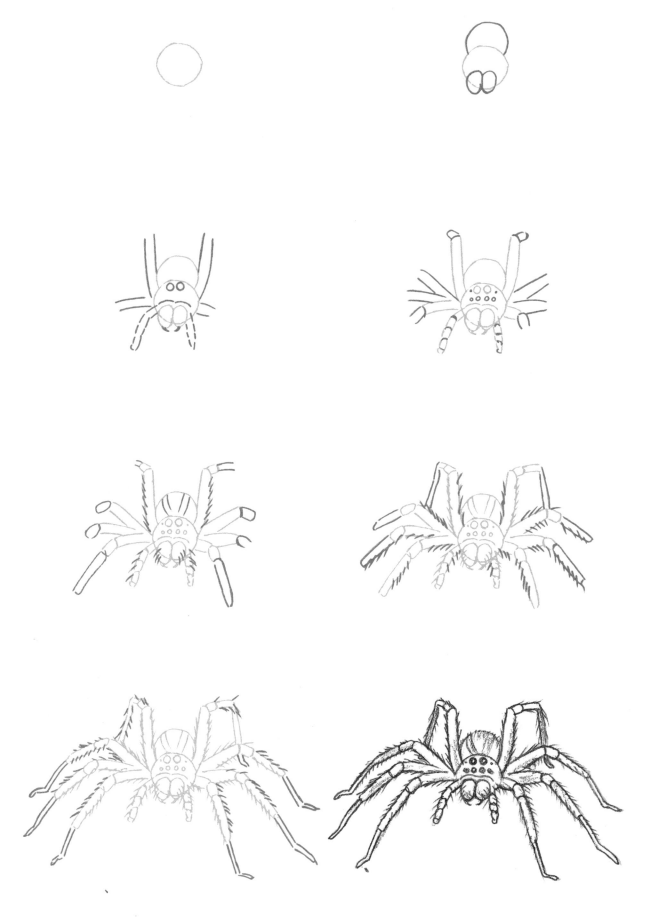

Wolf Spider

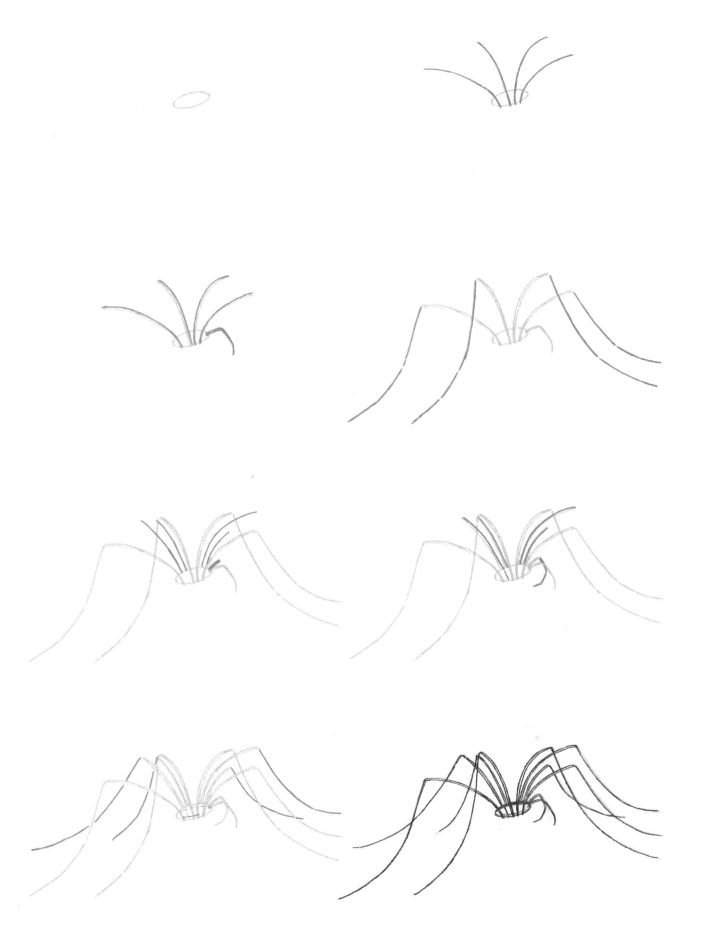

Daddy Longlegs

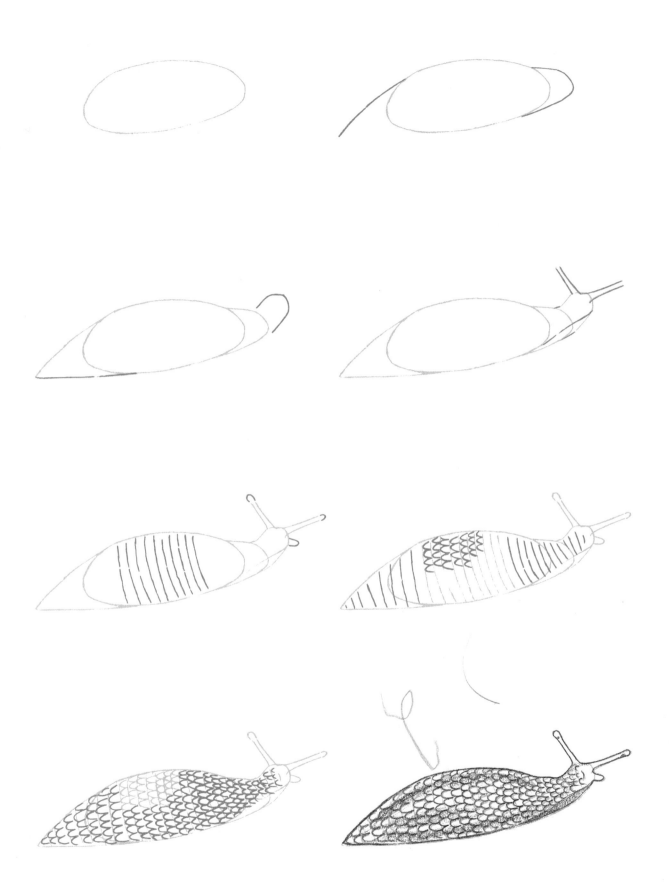

Slug

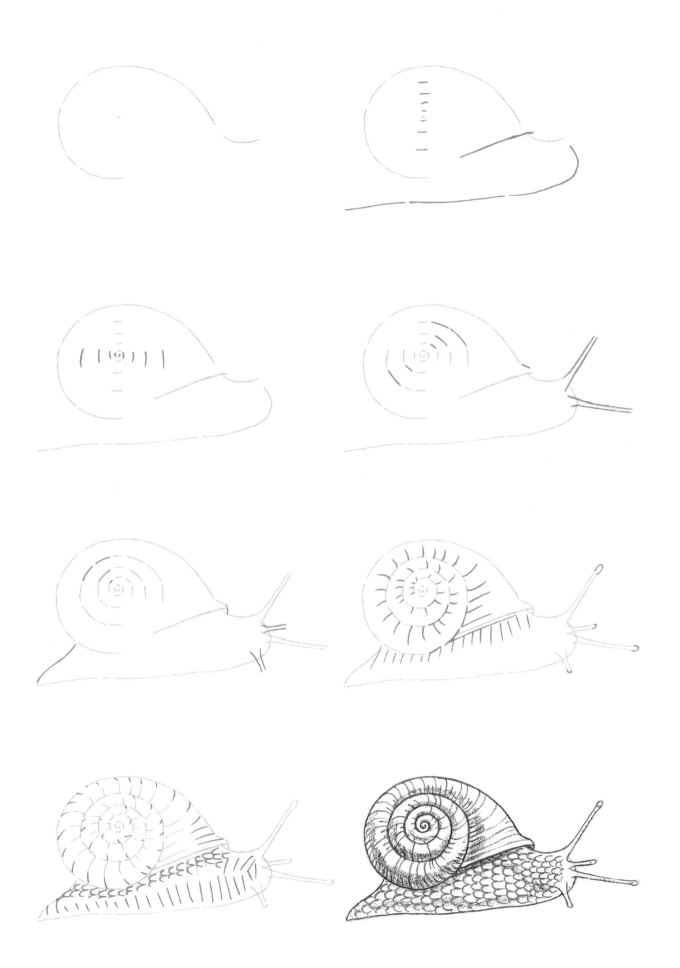

Snail

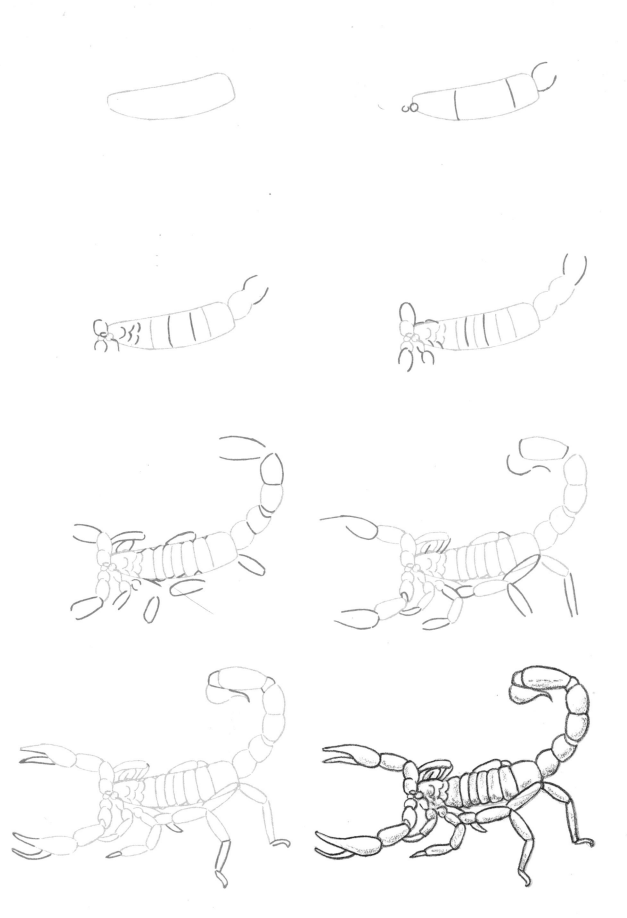

Scorpion

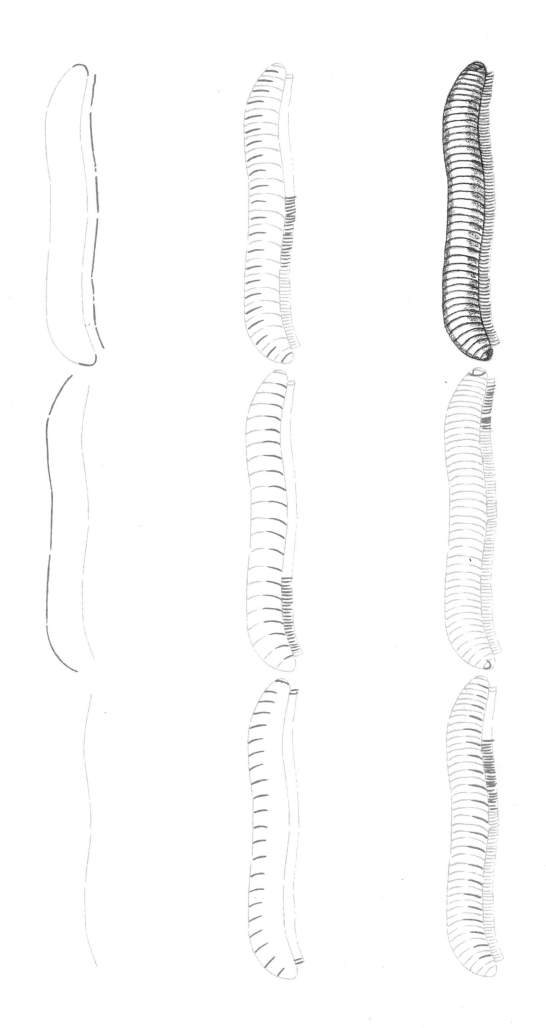

Millipede

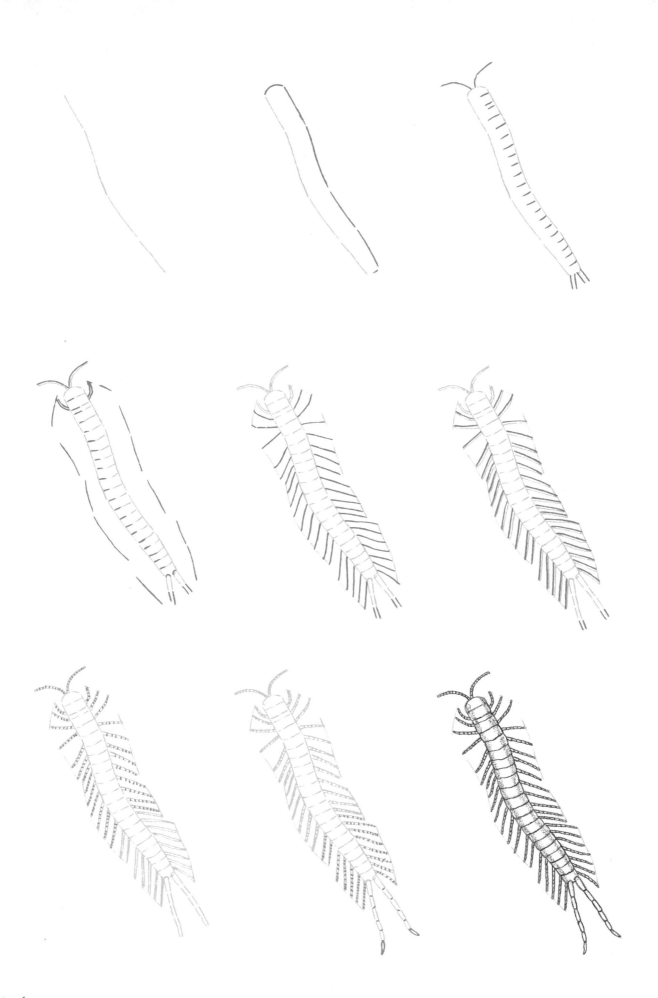

Centipede

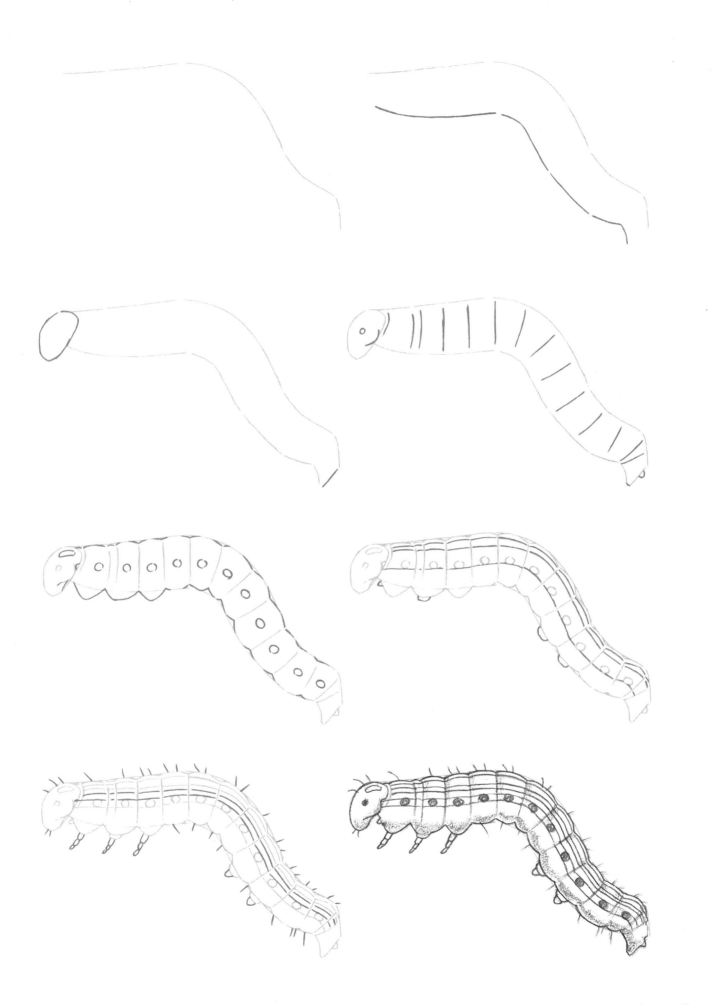

Caterpillar

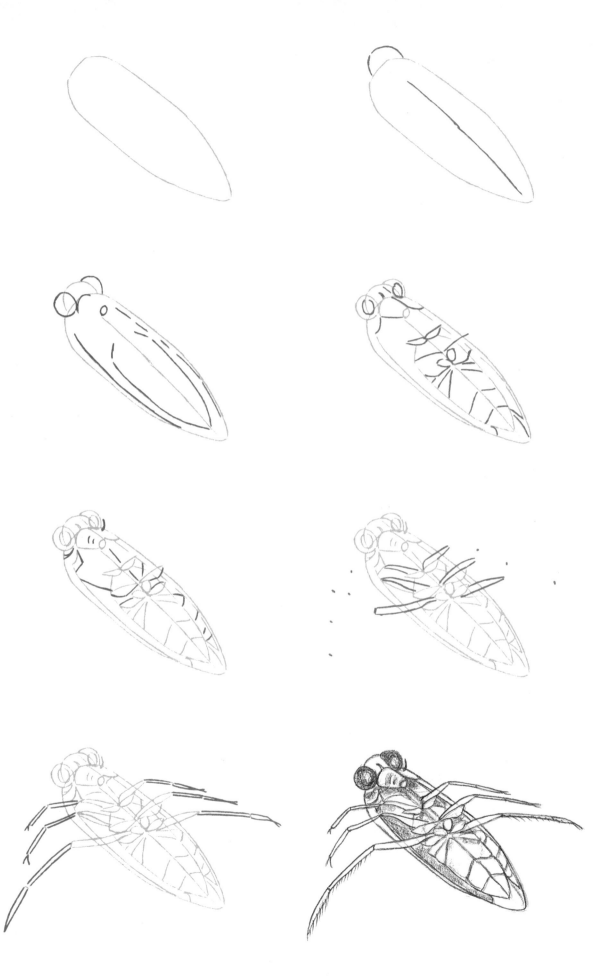

Back Swimmer

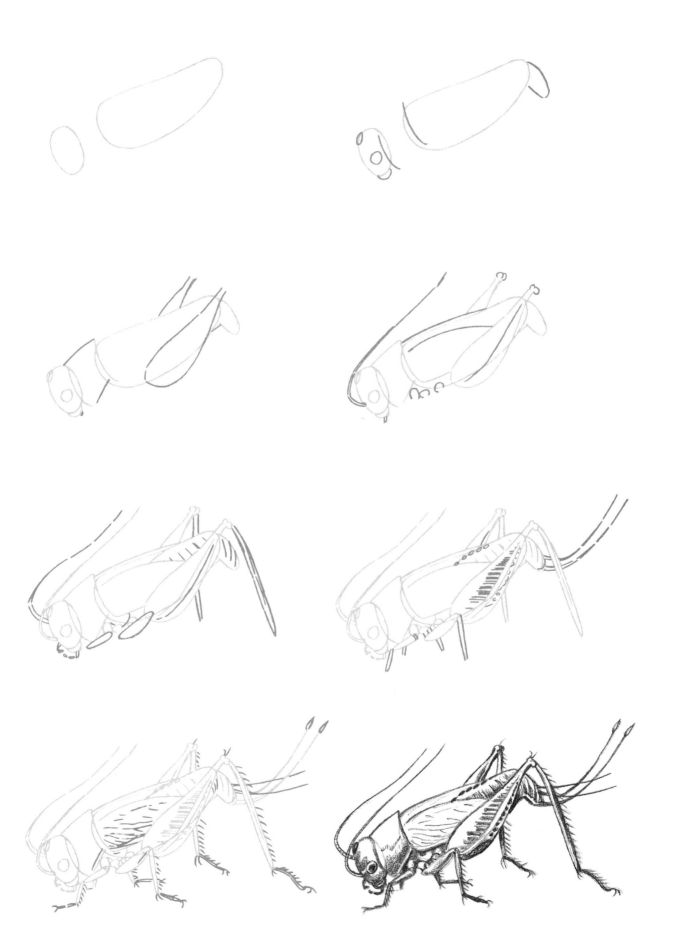

Field Cricket

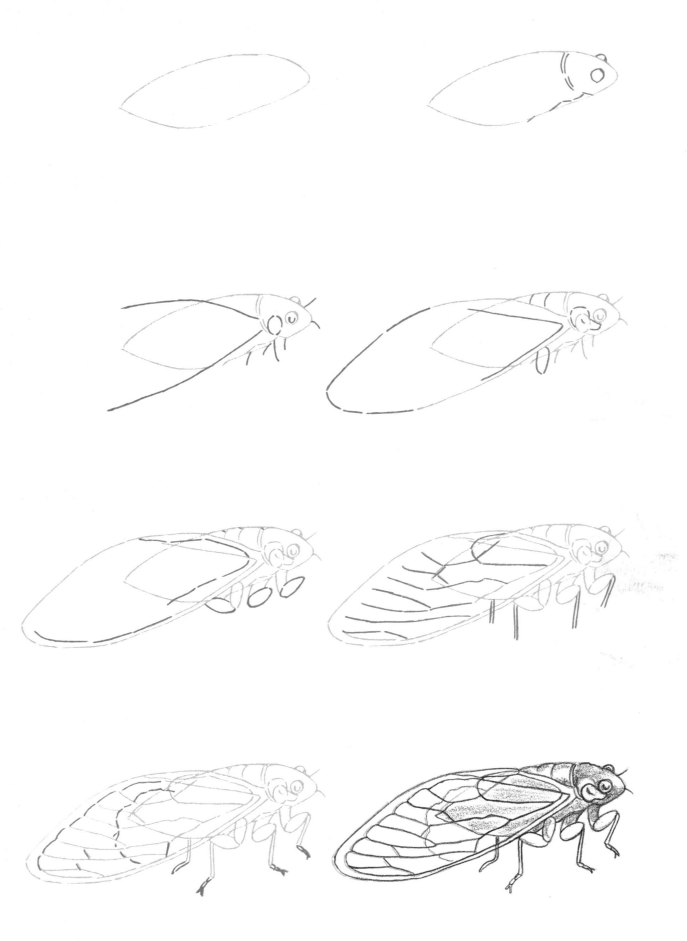

Cicada

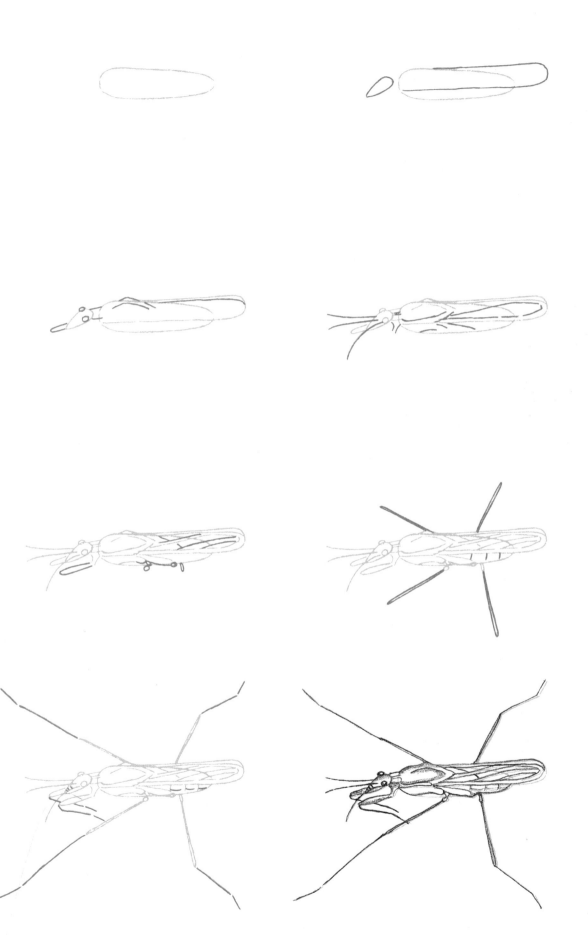

Water Strider

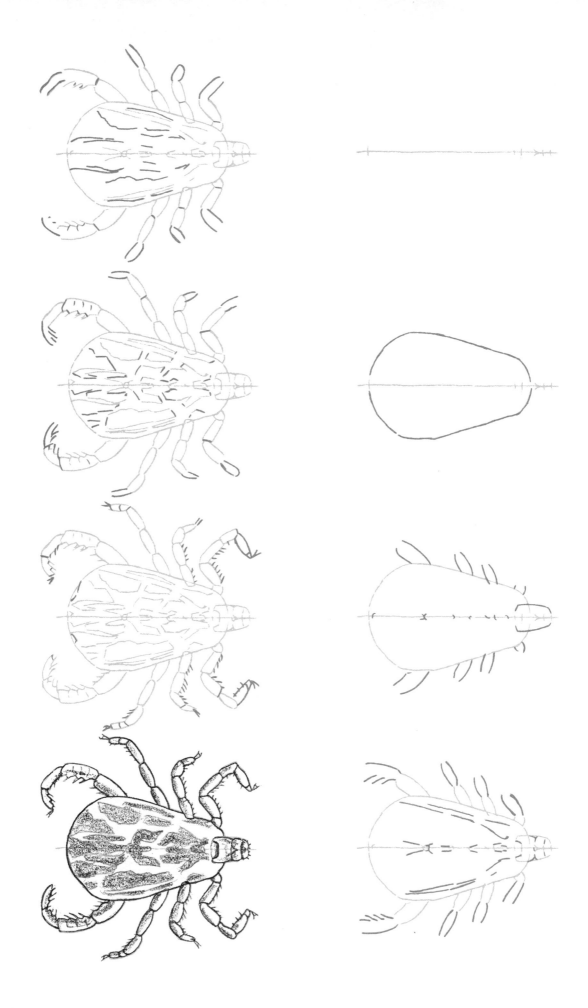

Lee J. Ames began his career at the Walt Disney Studios, working on films that included *Fantasia* and *Pinocchio*. He taught at the School of Visual Arts in Manhattan, and at Dowling College on Long Island, New York. An avid worker, Ames directed his own advertising agency, illustrated for several magazines, and illustrated approximately 150 books that range from picture books to postgraduate texts. He resided in Dix Hills, Long Island, with his wife, Jocelyn, until his death in June 2011.

Ray Burns began his career as a freelance illustrator in 1966, not only working as a cartoonist, but also illustrating nearly seventy children's books. An ex-naval officer, he also created storyboards for television.

DRAW 50 CREEPY CRAWLIES

Experience All That the Draw 50 Series Has to Offer!

With this proven, step-by-step method, Lee J. Ames has taught millions how to draw everything from amphibians to automobiles. Now it's your turn! Pick up the pencil, get out some paper, and learn how to draw everything under the sun with the Draw 50 series.

Also Available:

- *Draw 50 Aliens*
- *Draw 50 Animals*
- *Draw 50 Animal 'Toons*
- *Draw 50 Athletes*
- *Draw 50 Baby Animals*
- *Draw 50 Beasties*
- *Draw 50 Birds*
- *Draw 50 Boats, Ships, Trucks, and Trains*
- *Draw 50 Cats*
- *Draw 50 Cars, Trucks, and Motorcycles*
- *Draw 50 Dinosaurs and Other Prehistoric Animals*
- *Draw 50 Dogs*
- *Draw 50 Endangered Animals*
- *Draw 50 Famous Cartoons*
- *Draw 50 Flowers, Trees, and Other Plants*
- *Draw 50 Horses*
- *Draw 50 Magical Creatures*
- *Draw 50 Monsters*
- *Draw 50 People*
- *Draw 50 Princesses*
- *Draw 50 Sharks, Whales, and Other Sea Creatures*
- *Draw 50 Vehicles*
- *Draw the Draw 50 Way*